Painted in Blood,

MW00675959

The

Masterpiece

Sandy Davis Kirk, Ph.D.

McDougal Publishing is a ministry of The McDougal Foundation, Inc., a Maryland nonprofit corporation dedicated to spreading the Gospel of the Lord Jesus Christ to as many people as possible in the shortest time possible.

Published by:
McDougal Publishing
P.O. Box 3595
Hagerstown, MD 21742-3595
www.mcdougalpublishing.com

ISBN-13   978-1-58158-107-2

Printed in the United States of America
For Worldwide Distribution

Dedication

This book is dedicated to our interns and students around the world who burn to spread the glory of the Lamb to all the nations of this earth.

Acknowledgments

My heart fills with gratitude to all the pastors who've allowed us to bring the message of the Lamb to their people. My deep appreciation to Pastors Henry and Erica Schmidt, President of a ministry school in British Columbia, for teaching your students about the centrality of the Cross, preparing them for our teaching on the Lamb in the school. I thank God for Pastors Chris and Susan Clay and your beautiful family from Macclesfield, England. God is using you to spread the glory of the Lamb and His healing power all over the world. My deep appreciation goes to Pastors Peter, Julia, and Lydia Rooke for your passion for the Lamb and His presence in Dorchester. I thank our dear friends Pastors Rod and Michelle Smith in Poringland for your intense hunger for the Lamb and His love. I deeply appreciate Pastors David Miller and Graham Timson in Peterborough, England, where God's Spirit moves so powerfully.

I also thank Pastors Richard and Sheila Goddard from London, and Pastors Tim and Cara Griffith from south

London, and Pastors Mark and Sherryll Baines from Cambridge for your hunger for the Lamb and your openness to the presence of God in your churches.

Yes, at long last, the Lamb is being brought back to the center of His church on earth, even as He is in Heaven. And nothing so gratifies the heart of the Father as seeing His own pierced Son receive the reward He deserves for giving His life as a Lamb.

Contents

"Behold! The Lamb of God who takes away the sin of the world" (John 1:19 NKJ).

A Compelling Masterpiece
The Most Beautiful Sight in the World

A young man stands on a windswept hill outside Jerusalem. The view before him stuns his senses. His face flushes. Hot tears burn down his cheeks. His whole body trembles under the power of the visage before him. For here, flung up on two pieces of wood, exhibited before the eyes of all humanity, hangs Jesus Christ—God's eternal Son.

As this young disciple, whose name is John, looks up, he gazes upon the turning point of history. This is the apex of all time. The pinnacle. The mountain peak. It is the axis around which angels revolve. The supreme focus of Eternity. The heart of all Heaven.

This is God's love song without sound. His sermon without words. His dance without motion. His classic work of art. It is God's *Masterpiece,* painted in blood and floodlit with glory.

The Beauty of Jesus

In the little book you now hold in your hands, you

will look at Jesus as God's *Masterpiece*. As you look through John's eyes, you will find a forgotten part of the Easter story. Once you see it, you will behold the most beautiful sight in the world. It's like the story of the blind girl who reared her baby boy alone. She tried so hard to be the best mother she could to her child, but jobs were scarce and pay was low for blind people in those days.

As the child grew, he soon realized how much his mother suffered from her blindness. Often at night, when she tucked him in bed, he would say, "Mommy, someday when I'm big, I'm gonna buy you an operation for your eyes." Then with tears in his eyes, he would add, "So you can see me!"

Finally that day came and the young man led his blind mother into the hospital for an operation that could restore her sight. The surgery was performed and after days of waiting, the time came to remove the bandages. The young man sat anxiously holding his mother's hand as the doctor removed the bandages. When he lifted the gauze pads from her eyelids, her lashes fluttered. She blinked. Light struck her eyes and she flinched. But in moments she opened wide her eyes. . . and she could see!

Now, for the first time in her life, she looked into the face of her son. At first she couldn't speak. She just looked at him with tears flooding down her cheeks. Then a bright smile broke over her face, and she cried with all her heart,

"Oh, Son! You're the most beautiful sight in the whole world!"

In a far higher way, so is Jesus. He's the most beautiful sight you will ever behold, especially when you see what He did for you on the Cross. As one has said, "Since my eyes have looked on Jesus, I've lost sight of all beside; so enchained my spirit's vision, gazing on the Crucified."

You will find that "gazing on the Crucified" transforms your whole view of Christianity. Nothing so clears the vision, heals one's heart, stirs fire in the bones, breathes life into the human spirit, and burns passion into the soul as a long, steady gaze at God's Lamb. As Charles Spurgeon said, "There is life in a look at the Crucified!"[1]

Power of Beholding

Now as John looks up at Jesus, he wants to turn his gaze away, but he can't tear his eyes from this bleeding figure on the Cross. In his arms he holds Jesus' mother, Mary, as together they stand, looking up at this grisly but arresting sight.

A sense of reverence sweeps over John, filling him with longing. Like the tug of a magnet on metal filings, his heart feels drawn toward Jesus. He can't look away from the Lamb. It is just as Jesus said, *"But I, when I am lifted up from the earth will draw all men to myself"* (John 12:32).

This is indeed the wooing, inspiring, drawing power

of Christ lifted up on the Cross. It's the magnetism of Calvary. It is Deep calling unto deep. It is God's Compelling *Masterpiece.*

So come with me now to a tear-drenched hillside to gaze upon the Lamb. This time, however, let's look beyond the bleeding wounds. Let's see deeper than the physical pain of scourge and spikes and spear. Let's look with open heart into the depths of the Cross.[2] Let's see something we may have overlooked.

This is not a new revelation. It's an open secret. It has always been there, buried in the pages of the Bible. We didn't see it because we rarely heard it preached. Former generations were gripped by it, but somehow in our materialistic Western church, we missed it. In this postmodern age of prosperity, we've lost sight of this central truth in the Gospel.

It's time now to dig out a buried treasure. Time to look beyond the veil and view what angels dare to see.[3] It's time for God's Son to receive the glory He deserves for giving His life as a Lamb. Rather than bunnies and chocolate eggs, it's time for the glory of the Lamb to become the central focus of Easter.[4]

So open wide and let the eyes of your soul behold the beauty of the Lamb. Come gaze with all your heart on the most beautiful sight in the world — *The Masterpiece.*

Endnotes

1. Charles Spurgeon, "The Lamb of God," *Spurgeon's Expository Encyclopedia,* Vol. 12 (Grand Rapids, MI: Baker Book House, 1977), p. 487.

2. Although no one can ever fully plumb the depths of the meaning of the Cross of Jesus Christ, for an even closer look at the story of the Lamb than has been presented here, see my book *The Glory of the Lamb* (McDougal Publishing, 2004). This can be ordered from your favorite bookstore or from the Internet.

3. In Heaven, angelic beings gaze continually upon the slain Lamb of God (see Revelation 5:6-12).

4. I use this term "Easter" because although it is a pagan term, it is meaningful to so many people.

One

The Forgotten Masterpiece

Finding a Missing Truth in the Western Gospel

John's heart pounds wildly in his chest. Wind whips his tunic and scattered raindrops splash his cheeks, but he doesn't notice. He grips Mary a little tighter as together they look up at the towering *Masterpiece* on the hill.

Yes, here on this lonely mount called Calvary, God the Father has dipped His brush into the blood of His own Son. With tender touches of mercy and blazing strokes of judgment, He has painted His love on the canvas of His own Son's flesh. He has raised Him up on the easel of the Cross. Displayed Him in the gallery of Golgotha. Pulled back the veil and thundered through Heaven and earth — *"Behold the Lamb! He is forever the Masterpiece of God!"*

The Look in Jesus' Eyes

Lightning scorches the darkness, bathing the Lamb with

light. John sees the Master convulsing under the heavy weight of sin which infuses His whole being. With the onslaught of darkness, God has taken all the sins of humanity and thrust them upon His beloved Son.

The disciple swallows hard against the lump in his throat and brushes away tears with the back of his hand. He sees Jesus writhing and twisting under the crushing weight of sin. His wounded back and shoulders grind against the rough wood.

But suddenly Jesus' body stiffens. His face drains chalk white. Not a word falls from His lips. His frame tenses rigidly. His eyes are nearly swollen shut. They sink in their sockets, filled with tears and untold grief. His chest rises with each quick, shallow gasp.

The Master's body hangs frozen, paralyzed under the weight of something unimaginable. It's as though an unseen furnace has opened over Him and the Son has been cast like a lamb into the roasting flames.

John's heart feels raw and swollen. A nervous chill sweeps over him. Sweat slides down his neck and back. *What is happening to the Master?*

He doesn't know, but he feels the terror and destiny of the moment. He is beholding now the high point of the Cross. This is the forgotten glory of Easter. This is the crowning stroke of God's *Masterpiece* as the Father tips His Cup over Jesus....

John looks into the Master's face, grasping for understanding. His heart stands still at what he sees.

The look in Jesus' eyes is indescribable. His eyes are filled with horror. They speak of a mystery too deep for words.

I've seen that look before, thinks John. *Where was it? In the garden. . . Yes, just last night I heard Him praying and His eyes filled with this same look of terror….*

Terror in Gethsemane

Asleep on the moist ground of a garden on the Mount of Olives, a strange sound had shaken the young disciple awake. It was like a deep vibration, a strange force in the earth beneath him. He lifted his head and listened.

The air was still, cool, and crisp on this late night in spring. A bright Passover moon illumined the garden, casting silvery glints on the olive leaves.

There it was again. A deep moan. A loud masculine sob: "Father!"

It's Jesus! John realized with a start. *He's praying!* The young disciple crawled up closer, not wanting to disturb the Lord, but hungry to hear every word. Jesus had said, *"Pray with me, for I am grieved almost to the point of death"* (see Matthew 26:38).[1]

Yes, that's where I first saw that frantic look of fear in His eyes, thinks John. *Oh, Lord, You asked me to pray, but I was too weak. I fell asleep when You needed me.*

John clawed his way closer, longing to hear but afraid to look. As he gazed at the Lord in the bright light of the full moon, what he saw knocked the wind from his lungs.

The night was cold, but Jesus' body was bathed in sweat. *No! It's not just sweat – it's blood!*

John could not believe it. He squinted and peered out through the garden. He was only a stone's throw away, and now he could clearly see.

Blood coated the Master's face. Red splotches soaked His robe. Streams of bloody sweat pooled to the ground beneath Him, for *"His sweat was as it were great drops of blood falling down to the ground"* (Luke 22:44, KJV). The Greek for *"great drops"* is *thrombos*, signifying, "lumps or clots." Jonathan Edwards explained:

> The distress and anguish of his mind was so unspeakably extreme as to force his blood through the pores of his skin…so plentifully as to fall in great clots or drops from his body to the ground.[2]

John could see tears gushing from Jesus' eyes and blood pressing from His pores as He cried, *"Father, My Father, if it is possible, take away this Cup!"*

This Cup? What is this mysterious Cup? thought John.

Scriptures rolled through his mind: *"In the hand of the L*ORD *is A CUP full of foaming wine"* (Psalms 75:8). *"This CUP* [is] *filled with the wine of* [GOD'S] *WRATH,"* and all who drink it *"will stagger and go mad"* (Jeremiah 25:15-16). *"THE CUP from the L*ORD*'s hand is coming around to you, and disgrace will cover your glory"* (Habakkuk 2:16). *"See, I have taken out of your hand THE CUP that made you stagger…,the goblet of MY WRATH"* (Isaiah 51:22).[3]

The Cup Overflows

John's thoughts return now to the Cross. His pulse throbs wildly in his throat as he looks up at Jesus, for he realizes—*He is about to drink that Cup!*

Stand back now, John, and watch the Father's Cup of wrath pour down upon His beloved Son….

Now, like an erupting volcano in the heart of God, the Cup overflows and roars down upon the Lamb. The *"wine of God's fury, which has been poured full strength into the CUP OF HIS WRATH"* (Revelation 14:10), rushes down upon Him.

Jesus drinks and drinks and drinks. Every drop of consuming wrath pours over His tender soul, punishing Him for sin. Wave after pounding wave of judgment batters down upon Him. Over and over the wrath of God smashes His gentle heart. He is being *"STRICKEN BY GOD, SMITTEN by him and afflicted"*…. He is being *"CRUSHED for our iniquities; the PUNISHMENT that brought us peace* [is] *upon him"* (Isaiah 53:4-5).

John looks on, his own heart hammering in his head, as Jesus endures the flames of this eternal furnace. Images of the Passover lamb roasting over the fire fill him. He sees the burnt offering consumed on the altar of God. Flames from the burning bush leap up before his mind.

Yes, something of monumental proportion is happening as Jesus diverts the thunderbolts of divine judgment which we deserve for sin, taking this punishment upon himself. Arthur Pink explains that all the gnashing of teeth in the lake of fire will not compare with "the wrath of God which flamed against His Son on the cross."[4]

Through the Flames

Did you know that Jesus drank this Cup for you? Did you realize that He plunged through flames of wrath and hell so you could have eternal life?

It's like the story of Will Carter who drove into his driveway late one night, just in time to see flames shooting from the roof of his home. He jumped from his car and raced to the front door. Unlocking it, he began yelling for his wife. Not a sound. He tried to enter the house, but the entire downstairs was engulfed in flames. The intense heat drove him back outside.

By now fire trucks had arrived and a ladder was raised to an upstairs window. A firefighter charged up the ladder and broke through the glass. Then he took a long hose and began spraying the room inside.

All this time, the young man screamed, "My wife! My wife! She's pregnant. Somebody get her out!"

Finally, he could take it no longer. He grabbed hold of the ladder, climbed up and around the fireman, and dove through the open window. Thick black smoke filled the room, and flames filled the hallway, but he plunged through the burning to reach his beloved wife.

Reaching the bedroom, he saw her lying unconscious on the bed, suffocating from smoke inhalation. He threw himself over her and began breathing into her mouth, giving her all the air he could breathe into her failing lungs. Finally, she opened her eyes. Clutching her stomach she whispered weakly, "The baby, Will, the baby!"

Wrapping his wife in a blanket, he lifted her over his shoulder and fought his way back through the flames. Stumbling to the window, flames searing His flesh and burning to the bone, he placed her in the waiting firefighter's arms. Then he descended part way down the ladder and fell to the ground — *dead!*

The woman was rushed to the hospital where she gave birth to a healthy boy. She named him Will, after his dad. As the boy grew, he often listened as his mom told stories about his courageous father. Always she would say, "Will, because he went through the flames for you and me, we're alive today!"

That's what Jesus did for you. There in the garden, as He looked into the Father's Cup, He saw you! You were suffocating from the effects of sin. He saw you unconscious of the danger as the fire raged all around you. He saw what would happen if He did not drink the Father's Cup and rescue you from hell.

You say, "But I'm not so bad." Maybe not, but sin separates you from God. Sin cannot come into His holy presence. Sin must be punished. So that you could have eternal life in the presence of God, Jesus raced down to earth and threw Himself in front of the flames of God's wrath for you. Then He scooped you up, wrapped you in His love, and saved you from the fire. He brought you through to safety, and He forever bears the scars.

You see, this is the missing truth of the Western Gospel. That God's eternal Son took the punishment of hell which we deserve for our sins is the lost glory of Easter. It is God's forgotten *Masterpiece*. As the mother said to her son, "Because He went through the flames for you, you're alive today!"

Weeping for the Cross

One day in chapel at our "Glory of the Lamb" internship, I saw Michelle, an eighteen-year-old from England, weeping on her face, groaning and sobbing loudly. She was looking into the Father's Cup, and her heart was breaking for the Lamb. She was devastated as she saw what her sin had done to Jesus. And though she was a quiet, somewhat shy young lady who had never preached before in her life, when she rose from that floor, she was transformed. It was as if a volcano had erupted inside of her.

A few weeks later she stood before students at Evangel University in Missouri, preaching with a force and power such as I have rarely seen even from seasoned preachers. She described the depths of the Cup Jesus drank, her voice trembling with passion and fire. Her words seared right into the hearts of the students as they fell to their faces before God, weeping and wailing at the altar. One student, who had planned to end his life, cried, "Now at last I have a reason to live!"

I tell you there is a hidden power in the message of the Cross, which we have missed. Paul wrote, *"For the message of the cross. . . is the power of God"* (1 Corinthians 1:18). God is indeed unveiling the depths of His *Masterpiece*. He is causing us to discover the power of beholding the Lamb. It is the forgotten glory of Easter.

Yet most of us have cried more tears over the death of a pet than over the death of our Lord. Have you ever wept over the Cross? Have you looked into the contents of the Father's Cup until your heart melted in tears? Have you cried out with burning passion, pleading with the Father to bring His Son the reward of His suffering?

This is what He waits to hear. So won't you look up to Jesus even now? Tell Him how sorry you are for neglecting the Cross so long. Let Him feel your genuine sorrow. Pour tears of repentance upon His wounded feet. Pray something like this:

Oh Jesus, I never knew you drank the Cup for me! Forgive me, Lord! I've been so complacent about Your Cross. Sometimes I even thought I had suffered more than You. Oh God, I'm so sorry!

And now, with all my heart, I embrace Your Cross. Like the apostle Paul, I resolve to know nothing but Jesus Christ and him crucified (1 Corinthians 2:2). I promise that for the rest of my life I will explore the depths of your Cross and tell everyone about the beauty of GOD'S MASTERPIECE!

Endnotes

1. Mark wrote, *"He began to be deeply distressed and troubled"* (Mark 14:33); the Greek here is ekthambeô, meaning "horror-struck."
2. Jonathan Edwards, "Christ's Agony,"*The Works of Jonathan Edwards,* Vol.2 (Edinburgh: Banner of Truth Trust, 1995) p. 868.
3. British scholar John R. W. Stott explains: "This Old Testament imagery would have been well known to Jesus. He must have recognized the cup he was being offered as containing the wine of God's wrath" (*The Cross of Christ* [Downers Grove, IL: InterVarsity Press, 1986], p. 77).
4. A. W. Pink, *Seven Sayings of Christ on the Cross* (Grand Rapids, MI: Baker Book House, 1958), p. 72.

   This is what great theologians say about Jesus enduring hell on the Cross: John R. W. Stott said, we may "dare to say our sin sent Christ to hell…before his body died." Then Stott explains that this was not to *hades,* the abode of the dead, but to *gehenna,* the place of eternal punishment (*The Cross of Christ,* p. 79).

   Charles Spurgeon wrote, "O hell, with all thine infinite horrors and flames unquenchable, and pains and griefs and shrieks of tortured ghosts, even thou canst not reveal the justice of God as Christ revealed it in His riven heart upon the bloody tree" (Charles Spurgeon, *Twelve Sermons on the Passion and Death of Christ* [Grand Rapids, MI: Baker Book House, n.d.], p. 55).

   Referring to Jesus' words about being sorrowful "even unto death," Jonathan Edwards said that this seems "to intimate that the very pains and sorrows of hell, of eternal death, had got hold of him…. Christ suffered that which…was fully equivalent to the misery of the damned, for it was the wrath of the same God" ("Christ's Agony," *The Works of Jonathan Edwards,* Vol. 2 [Edinburgh: Banner of Truth Trust, 1995], p. 868a, 871b). Jonathan Edwards also wrote, "The bush burning with fire represented the sufferings of Christ in the fire of God's wrath" ("The History of the Work of Redemption," *The Works of Jonathan Edwards,* Vol. 1 [Edinburgh: Banner of Truth Trust, 1995], p. 546).

Two

The Forsaken Masterpiece

Receiving a Passion for God's Son as the Lamb

A flurry of warm tears wells up in John's eyes, but he fights to choke back his emotions. *For Mary's sake, I must hold myself together,* he thinks.

Jesus looks utterly forsaken by God, as deeper and deeper He plunges into the abysmal depths of His wrath. Finally, He can take no more. He throws back His head and pushes down on the spike in His feet in order to fill His lungs with air.

Pain claws John's heart as he watches the wound in Jesus' feet rip open. He and Mary edge in a little closer to the Cross, straining to hear every word. Then it happens…

The Cry of the Ages

Jesus lifts up His voice in an almost inhuman cry: *"Eli, Eli, lama sabachthani? My God, My God, why have You forsaken Me?"*

The blood-chilling howl shatters the silence at Calvary. It rips through the skies and pierces every heart like the sharp slash of the blade of a sword. Men and women gasp in shock. Angels stand aghast. All of nature holds its breath.

This gushing torrent of agony stuns the young disciple. Fear blinds him. Terror rises in his heart. The whole world spins as the cry of Jesus reels through his head. *How could the Son scream such words of rejection to His beloved Father?*

John, don't you know? It's because His soul is engulfing every drop of the Father's Cup. This cry gives us a window into His suffering. It is the most profound cry ever heard in Heaven or earth.

It reveals the wounded heart of the Son of God. His body has been flayed in pieces like a lamb for the sacrifice, but now His heart is being flayed into bloody shreds. It feels as though His soul is being cut up and consumed by God's eternal wrath, burned in the fiery waves of judgment that we deserve for sin. What's more, He bears this punishment alone.

Now this horrific cry from the Savior's lips, blazes up through the darkness and lands in the heart of God. The Father groans. He grips His heart and bends over in grief. In that holy moment, as angels hide their eyes in silence, the heart of the Father breaks. And as His heart tears, the veil in the temple is torn in two from top to bottom.

John stands frozen with fear. He feels as though his heart has been stabbed and torn by this piercing cry of the Lord. It's as if a veil has been ripped from his soul even as the veil in the temple was torn.

Pierced by His Cry

Now, if you will let this cry of Jesus pierce your own heart, it will tear a veil from the temple of your soul as well. One day I was teaching 400 teens at a Methodist youth camp about the power of the Cross. Together we looked up at Jesus. We saw His arms stretched out and riveted to a beam of wood. We saw the tears slipping down His cheeks, mixing with spittle and blood. We watched the Roman scourge rip into His flesh. We heard His last words. But when we heard His cry, *"Eli, Eli, lama sabachthani? My God, My God, why have You forsaken Me?"* something amazing happened in the room.

The Lord had shown me that if I would release this cry in a deep guttural roar, like Jesus cried it,[1] He would rip veils from people's hearts. And that's exactly what He did with hundreds of complacent teenagers. As I was about to release this hideous cry, I took a deep breath; then, with a loud, animal-like roar, I bellowed: *"Eli, Eli, lama sabachthani? My God, My God, why have You forsaken Me?"*

Suddenly the Holy Spirit swept in and filled the whole room with His presence. It was like a baptism of fire, falling upon the kids. Strong teenage boys shook with emotion, their faces flushing with the glory of God, their bodies trembling in His presence. Precious young girls sobbed openly as the Holy Spirit burned down upon them. It was overwhelming, and it led to many giving their lives to Christ.

What was it that opened Heaven and released such a flood of God on these apathetic teens? It was hearing again the cry of Jesus. The same cry that broke God's heart, tore open the veil, and shattered the earth, ripped veils from the temple of their hearts.

Now for the past twenty years I've been teaching and writing and pouring into students about the depths of the Cross, especially the Father's Cup.[2] Through the years, I've seen the Holy Spirit etch deep scars of love on the hearts of hundreds of students. One young woman said, "I'm a pastor's kid, but my heart was unmoved by the Cross. Then I looked inside the Father's Cup, and my heart has never stopped trembling."

I've heard so many students cry, "God has pierced my heart for the Lamb!" "Something inside me burns for the Cross of Jesus Christ!" "I promise that for the rest of my life I will only preach Jesus Christ and Him crucified!" But it was gazing deeply into the Cup Jesus drank which opened their eyes and scarred their hearts for the Lamb.

I saw this happen in a "Glory of the Lamb" class at our internship one morning. With gushing passion, I roared this deep, guttural cry of Jesus. All over the room young adults hit the floor, wailing and weeping before God. It was as though the Holy Spirit took His sword and chiseled the mark of the cross into their hearts.

Later, Brandon told how his own heart had been pierced while he was playing the role of Jesus in a drama at our camp. A group from an inner-city mission sat in our prayer garden under the oak trees, watching the drama. Brandon had been beaten by soldiers and now hung on the Cross, covered with blood. Then he lifted up his voice and screamed at the top of his lungs, *"Eli, Eli, lama sabachthani? My God, My God, why have You forsaken Me?"* The words shook every heart, but most of all, they shook Brandon. He said, "It was like my heart tore open and a fire poured in. I still feel the burning!"

A Passion for God's Son

One night I heard four of our interns from England praying in a corner of the chapel. I slipped over and listened as they poured out their hearts. Sophie cried, "Oh, Jesus, You drank the Cup for me! You cried that cry for me!" Michelle prayed, "Father, this is Your Son! Your Son!" Mandy wept, "Oh Father, how can we bring Him His reward in England? People have forgotten Your Son! Even in America—in the church—people have forgotten the Lamb!"

As they prayed with all the passion of their hearts, their faces reddened, tears streamed down their cheeks, and their bodies rocked back and forth. I was melted by their prayers, for I knew they had touched the Father's heart for His Son. They were crying out to bring Jesus the reward of His suffering.

Yes, this is what the Father waits to see. He longs for a generation to arise whose hearts will burn for His Son's sacrifice. He yearns for God's forsaken *Masterpiece* to be lifted up for all to see. He longs to see Easter transformed from a time of candy and eggs to a time of honoring the Lamb for what He suffered on the Cross.

But not just at Easter—all year long! He wants to see men and women arise, releasing the cry of forsakenness to the earth, so that at last, people will know that they are never forsaken by God. He waits for a generation to step forward and tell about the blazing Cup of wrath He endured for them.

The Forgotten Baby

Jonathan Edwards said that Jesus' chief purpose for going to the Cross was "to drink that cup."[3] Yet in today's postmodern church, we rarely hear it mentioned. Once a year at Easter we may bring the Cross out of the shadows, but do we ever look into the Father's Cup?

We're much like the mother who left her baby in the car on a hot summer day. She ran into the store to pick up a few groceries, but once inside, she remembered all the things she needed and she forgot about the baby. Friends stopped and talked to her and time slipped away. By the time she paid for her groceries, over an hour had passed. As she pushed the cart toward her car, she suddenly gasped, "My baby! My baby!" Frantically she rushed to the car, fumbled for her keys, and unlocked the door. But it was too late. The baby lay slumped over his car seat, dead from suffocation.

But that's what we've done in the church! We've forgotten the Baby! Of course we love the Cross, the place of our salvation, but have we ever taken the time to look into the depths of what our Jesus did for us? We run to conferences, buying countless CDs about blessings and prosperity. We listen for hours to messages on miracles, glory, and power, but all of these blessings flow down from the Lamb.

In spite of all the good messages and all our great programs, we've missed the full glory of Easter. We've suffocated the Baby in the midst of His own church. Let's not allow all the trappings of Easter to obscure the Baby any longer. Let's open our eyes, pull back the veil, and display in every way possible *The Masterpiece*.

Even more, let's bare our souls to the Lamb and ask Him to pierce our hearts with the sword of the Lord. His sword is His Word, but the tip of the blade is the message of the Cross and the point is His heart-rending cry, *"My God, My God, why have You forsaken Me?"*

Even now, ask Him to come and take you to the Cross. Gaze up at Jesus and pray:

Oh God, I lay my heart bare before Your sword. I gaze into the depths of Your Cross and hear again Your piercing cry.

Come, Holy Spirit, and drive that cry into my heart. Let me feel it to the core of my being. Let my heart bear the scar of Your piercing so that never again will I allow God's Baby to be suffocated in the church. With all my heart I will live to display GOD'S FORSAKEN MASTERPIECE.

Endnotes

1. This was the cry of Psalm 22:1, which says, *"My God, my God, why have you forsaken me? Why are you so far from saving me, so far from the words of my groaning?"* In Hebrew, the word *"groaning,"* is *sheagah*, meaning "a rumbling, moaning, mighty roaring." That's why this cry of Jesus is called "the cry of dereliction."
2. For five years I taught seven different courses at the ministry school from the Brownsville Revival. In every course, whether Old Testament, New Testament, or Systematic Theology, every subject led back to the Cross. Now we've started a three-month "Glory of the Lamb" internship at our camp, for people who hunger to go deeper in the Lamb.
3. Jonathan Edwards, "Christ's Agony," *The Works of Jonathan Edwards*, Vol. 2 (Edinburgh: Banner of Truth Trust, 1995) p. 867.

Three

The Victorious Masterpiece
Receiving Authority Over the Kingdom of Darkness

Tension crackles in the air at Calvary. John's throat feels raw and swollen with emotion. The cry of Jesus thunders soundlessly in his head.

The crowd stands petrified. Not a muscle moves. Not a breath or a shuffle. Even the moans of the women and the groans of the two thieves cease.

Jesus calls for a drink and a soldier lifts a sponge of cheap wine vinegar up to His lips. Now with His tongue moistened, the Master prepares to shout—not a cry of defeat, but a transcendent cry of victory.

John's heart leaps. Still holding Mary, he staggers back a step and watches Jesus. He sees a strange glint in the Master's eyes. *What is this? Fear no longer fills His eyes, for this is a look of triumph!*

The Cosmic Power Encounter

Yes, John, all this time, unseen by human eyes, a cosmic power encounter rages. Here on the battlefield of Calvary, the conflict of the ages between Christ and the kingdom of darkness takes place.

At the head of the ranks of evil stands Satan himself. He smirks, thinking he's got Jesus just where he wants Him. Ah, such sweet revenge! This is the One who humiliated him long ago, casting him out of Heaven to the earth (see Isaiah 14). Now this Son of God is getting what He deserves as He hangs in utter defeat, forsaken even by His Father.

"As he was suspended there, bound hand and foot to the wood in apparent weakness," writes Bible scholar F.F. Bruce, the forces of evil "imagined they had him at their mercy, and flung themselves upon him with hostile intent."[1]

What Satan doesn't understand, however, is that his only ground of attack on God's Son is sin. Because the Father has poured our sin on Jesus, Satan and all his minions have a legal right to attack Him. But they don't comprehend the divine mystery hidden since before the creation of the world. They don't know that the Lamb has agreed to drink His Father's Cup of wrath—punishing and annihilating sin *in Him!*

Yes, as Jesus drinks the last bitter drops of the Father's Cup, sin is annihilated in Him. As the Bible says, *"He has appeared once for all at the end of the ages to DO AWAY with sin by the sacrifice of himself"* (Hebrews 9:26). Another version says: He has come *"to ABOLISH sin by the sacrifice of himself"* (Hebrews 9:26, TCNT).[2]

Now, with the Father's Cup consumed, sin is fully punished, and Satan has no more hold on Jesus. As with Haman, hanged on his own gallows (see Esther 7), the very instrument on which Satan meant to kill the Savior has defeated him. As Martin Luther put it, Satan has fallen into the trap. The One who looks like *"a worm and not a man"* (Ps. 22:6), has dangled on the Cross, and like a greedy fish, Satan has gobbled the bait. Now he is hooked in the jaw, ensnared by God on the Cross.[3]

And though men have marred Jesus' flesh with spittle and thorns, drawn His blood with scourge and spikes, and thousands of principalities and powers have sunk poisonous fangs into His body, they are no match for the Lord of Glory.

The battle has been hot and the dust thick, but it is almost over. Satan rears back and hurtles forward, rushing like a battering ram in one last charge against the Lamb.

But what is this? There is no more sin for him to feed on! Jesus has fully consumed the final dregs of the Cup, and sin is obliterated in Him. Now Satan slams his head against the heel of Christ's foot … and his neck breaks. He falls, crushed beneath the feet of the Seed of the Woman (see Genesis 3:15).[4]

Now all the demons fall, vanquished—stripped, exposed, defeated—around their head-crushed leader. There they lie, in a heap beneath the feet of the Lamb.

A wild rush of anguish sweeps over John. He doesn't understand what is happening, but now Jesus, with tongue moistened, prepares to give the final shout of victory.

The Master pushes down with all His might on the spike in His feet to raise His chest for air. The wound in His feet tears open and blood trickles down, dripping on the demonic forces beneath Him. The blood of the Lamb splashes over them and they gag and gasp in utter defeat.

Yes, at long last the victory is won at Calvary, for Christ has come *"to destroy the devil's works"* (1 John 3:8). He overcame him, not in some mythical battle in hell after the Cross—but ON THE CROSS. It is just as the Bible says, *"Having disarmed the powers and authorities, he made a public spectacle of them, triumphing over them BY THE CROSS"* (Colossians 2:15).

Now hear the triumphant sixth word explode from the Conqueror's lips: *"It is finished!"* The Greek is *tetelestai*, in the perfect tense, meaning "that it has been and will forever remain finished."

The words of victory blast from the Champion's lips like the sound of rams' horns at the Feast of Trumpets. They resound across the hillside, jolting every heart, shaking the very gates of hell. They flash through the young disciple's mind and burn like fire in his heart.

John stands amazed, vibrating all over with the power of God. He doesn't fully understand it all yet, but the ring in the Master's voice and the look on His face, like the red flush of victory after a long and decisive battle, tells the young disciple that something of infinite significance has taken place.

Yes, John, an eternal victory has indeed been won, and now at last the *Masterpiece* is finished. The Master Artist prepares to lay His brush aside. The greatest work in all of human history is done. Even as God finished His work of creation on the sixth day, He now finishes His work of redemption with the sixth word.

Now the Father's Cup of eternal wrath is drained.[5] Sin is fully punished. The types and prophecies of the Old Testament are fulfilled. And a new covenant is cut in the flesh of God's own Son.

Furthermore, death is now conquered in Him, for Jesus has come to *"destroy him who holds the power of death – that is, the devil"* (Hebrews 2:14). Disease is overcome, for on the Cross He *"took up our infirmities"… and by his wounds* [we]*have been healed"* (Isaiah 53:45; 1 Peter 2:24). Now the spiritual David has cut off the giant's head, using Goliath's own sword (see I Samuel 17:51).

So, John, stand back now and look up at your Conquering King upon the throne. Now the bleeding Worm has become the blazing Warrior! The impotent One has become the Omnipotent One! The tortured Lamb is now the triumphant Lion! The suffering Victim has become the successful Victor!

Yes, the Cross of misery has become a Cross of Majesty as the King sits upon His throne. As John Calvin said, "There is no tribunal so magnificent, no throne so stately, no show of triumph so distinguished, no chariot so elevated" as is the Cross "on which Christ has subdued death and the devil and trodden them under his feet."[6]

John sees the blush of victory still glowing on Jesus' face as He shouts His last words from the Cross. Now the Master Artist lays down His brush. Even as God rested on the seventh day, He enters His rest with His seventh word.

Suddenly, thunder cracks and lightning lashes the sky, spotlighting the scene again. John and Mary stand mute with awe, transfixed by the compelling scene. Here, silhouetted in bold relief against the black backdrop of nature's fury, jutting upward like a grand monument, is the most awe-inspiring spectacle ever seen by human eyes—God impaled on a Cross!

Lightning strikes again and the ground begins to rumble. It almost seems the whole universe is responding to this divine conquest at Calvary. Floodlights of lightning. Cymbals of clashing thunder. Trumpets of howling wind. And drum rolls of rumbling earth. It's as though Almighty God is announcing with cosmic fanfare—"Behold the grand success of the Lamb! He is forever My Victorious *Masterpiece*!"

Victory at the Cross

Oh, John, no wonder you and the early church could *"trample on snakes and scorpions and … overcome all the power of the enemy"* (Luke 10:9). This is why you could write so confidently, *"They overcame him by the blood of the Lamb"* (Revelation 12:11).

And no wonder the apostle Paul could take his stand *"against the devil's schemes* [and] *against the rulers, against the authorities, against the powers of this dark world and against the spiritual forces of evil in heavenly realms"* (Ephesians 6:11-12).This is why he could say, *"No, in all these things we are more than conquerors through him who loved us"* (Romans 8:37).

Yes, John, you and the early church had seen something in the Cross that we've missed today. You understood that because wrath engulfed the Lamb,because sin was abolished, and because Satan was decisively defeated, you had authority over sin, sickness, death, and the devil. Your authority came from the finished work of the Cross.[7]

I could hardly believe what happened after our interns got hold of this forgotten truth. Once the Cup had burned open their hearts, a passion roared inside them which could not be contained. And once they saw the authority which Jesus died to give them, they were like *"calves released from the stall"* (Malachi 4:2).

In the midst of three intensive months of training, we sent them out on mission trips. When they returned, they were bursting to tell what happened. Eighteen-year-old Miranda told of being in Mexico, where she prayed for a lady whose arm had been broken two years before and had healed improperly, causing constant pain. "I couldn't understand her Spanish, but the Lord told me to pray for her arm. All of a sudden I heard bones crunching as they shifted back into place!" Excitedly she said, "I called for an interpreter and found that God had completely healed her arm with no more pain!"

Glen's voice broke as he said, "In the mountains I saw the Holy Spirit fall on little Mexican children." Aaron cried jubilantly, "Everyone I prayed for got healed!" Trevor said, "The Lord gave me a word of knowledge about a lady with a cataract. After prayer, the cataract fell off and she could see perfectly!" Miranda added, "We didn't know what we were doing, but as we stepped out in faith, God did it!"

On a university campus, Nic and Mark prayed for a football player who had torn cartilage in his leg. God healed him, and he stripped off his brace and jumped out of his wheelchair. The power of God came on him so strongly that he began praying for all of his friends. The next day, this popular boy stood on a chair in the cafeteria and said, "Look, guys, you know I don't normally do this, but God is real! Look what He did for my leg!"

You see, it's not about miracles to build our ministries or pack our churches. It's about lifting up the Lamb of God so He can receive the glory He deserves for what He suffered on the Cross. Signs and wonders simply point to the Lamb. They show us God's *Masterpiece*. For not only have we overlooked the Father's Cup, but we've also neglected the authority Jesus died to give us.

So, even now, look up to the Lamb of God. See the One who conquered fear, depression, disease, death, and the devil. Behold the Lamb who abolished sin in Himself. See the One who defeated Satan, crushing his head beneath His bleeding feet. Gaze on your conquering Hero — the Victorious *Masterpiece* of God.

Cry out to Him with all your heart:

Dear Jesus, I look up to Your finished work on the Cross to receive Your authority over evil. I'm so sorry I've lived in such defeat. Come, Holy Spirit, and fill me with Your power to lift high the glory of the Lamb. Flood me with Your authority to trample over demons, disease, and the devil, bringing them all under the bleeding feet of Christ. Grace me with the anointing which Jesus died to give me, so that I can show to the world — GOD'S VICTORIOUS MASTERPIECE!

Endnotes

1. E. K. Simpson and F. F. Bruce, *Commentary on the Epistles to the Ephesians and Colossians, New International Version Commentary on the New Testament* (Grand Rapids, MI: Wm. B. Eerdmans Publishing Company, 1957) p. 239.
2. TCNT refers to the *Twentieth Century New Testament.* (Moody Bible Institute).
3. Gustaf Aulen, *Christus Victor* (New York: MacMillan Publishing Company, 1969), pp. 103-104.
4. God said to Satan, *"I will put enmity between you and the woman, and between your offspring and hers; he will crush your head, and you will strike his heel"* (Genesis 3:15). This is called by scholars the *Protoevangelium*, which is considered the first proclamation of the Gospel.
5. It is only drained for those who will accept Christ and His sacrifice, for Revelation 14: 10 tells us that the Cup of wrath will be poured out on all who reject Christ and worship the beast.
6. John Calvin, *Institutes of the Christian Religion*, Vol. 1 (Grand Rapids, MI: Wm B. Eerdmans Publishing Company, 1983), Book II, p. 440.
7. In his classic book, *Christus Victor*, Gustaf Aulen tells how the early church and church Fathers clearly understood the victory of Christ on the Cross. They saw Jesus as triumphing over "sin, death, hell, and Satan." But this understanding faded out during the Dark Ages of the church. Martin Luther revived a victorious theology of the Cross during the Reformation, but eventually Protestant scholasticism clouded the clear revelation of the power and the victory of the Cross (Gustaf Aulen, *Christus Victor*, pp. 128-133).

Four

The Masterpiece of Glory
Drinking Deeply of His Resurrection Power

Rain at Calvary still drizzles, washing over the riddled body of Jesus. A soldier seizes a ladder and a crowbar, climbing up to the middle Cross. John's feelings jam in his throat as he watches rough hands pry the spike from Jesus' lifeless palm. The sight knocks the wind from John's chest.

Quickly, he tries to shield Mary from the view. "Come, Mary, it's time to go," he whispers raggedly. She nods as together they turn to leave. John looks back over his shoulder as soldiers slowly lower the body of Jesus to the arms of Joseph of Arimathea.

Mary sees it, too, and breaks from John's arms, rushing to the body of her Son. She falls on her knees as Joseph lays Him across her lap. She cradles his head and wails out her grief in loud Jewish abandon. John kneels beside her until the wailing subsides and she quietly weeps in his arms.

Finally, they rise and make their way, arm in arm, down the rocky slope. But suddenly, the moaning of the wind ceases. The drizzle stops. Black clouds scatter. Golden shafts of light streak across the western sky.

John pauses to take in the scene. A hush settles over the land. A soft breeze drifts over the hillside. The pungent scent of the earth after a fresh rain permeates the air. The smoky aroma of the evening sacrifice at three o'clock wafts through the vale. A bird sings. A snake slithers out from under a rock, as though it's been hiding.

John looks back one last time. Jesus' body has been removed for burial, but there in the distance, rising like a sun-splashed mountain peak against the azure sky, is the empty Cross of Jesus. The place where the most monumental work of all time has now been accomplished.[1]

This is indeed God's *Masterpiece* of Glory.

The Risen Masterpiece

For the next two nights, sleep seems impossible for John. He tosses fitfully on his pallet, but he doesn't know that over in the garden where Jesus was buried, something marvelous is about to happen….

In the early morning hours of the third day,[2] while darkness still pervades the land, suddenly, the leaves in the trees begin to rustle. A wind blows into the garden. Olive and almond leaves stir and gleam in the brightness of this supernatural current, for it's not a wind at all. It's the Person of the Holy Spirit, breezing into the garden like a gust of wind.

Toward the rock-hewn grave He rushes. Reaching the boulder which blocks the entrance, He whiffs through the rock and enters the tomb. For a moment He hesitates, looking down on the corpse of the One He loves, laid out on the slab.

His feelings are deep, for He is not a force. He is a Person. He is God, equal with the Father and the Son. He was with His Beloved One before the creation of the world in timeless, spaceless Infinitude. But the Holy Spirit is the One in the Godhead who possesses such extravagant tenderness. His feelings are exquisitely delicate. The Bible compares Him to a dove because He is gentle and easily grieved.

That's why, as God the Son hung convulsing in pain on the Cross, the Holy Spirit stood back moaning and weeping, rolling and writhing in unthinkable grief. He longed to run to His Beloved and wrap Him in His comforting wings, but He could not. This was a mission planned in the Godhead before the world's creation.[3]

But now, the work of the Cross is finished, and the precious Holy Spirit has ached for this moment. Closer now He draws to the body of the Son. He hovers above Him, waiting for the Father's command.

"Now, Holy Spirit!" shouts the Father, with tears bursting in His heart. "Raise My Son from the dead!"

With a mighty rush, the Holy Spirit sweeps into the lifeless frame of the Lamb. His presence floods Jesus' spirit …then His soul,…then His body. Glory pumps through every vein. The breath of God fills every part.

Now Jesus' heart begins to beat. He catches His breath and air fills His lungs. Oxygen surges through His body. Strength pours into His muscles. His eyelids flicker and He opens wide His eyes.

Slowly now He rises, lifting out of the grave clothes that wrapped His body. These clothes, deprived now of the body, sink in as if by the suction of a vacuum.

Jesus stands upright. He breathes out and glory floods the whole tomb. The rarefied air in the cave is thick with the presence of God.

Angels attending the glory fall backwards, trembling under *"the power outflowing from His resurrection"* (Philippians 3:10, AMP). They cover their eyes from the brilliance, for this is the resurrection power of the Lamb, now released from its storehouse. Glory floods out from Him like the waters spilling over Niagara Falls.

Jesus Appears

The sun is just beginning to peek above the eastern horizon in Israel as John awakens with a start. Bursting through the door of the upper room, Mary Magdalene cries, *"I have seen the Lord!"*

The young disciple gasps. Without hesitation, he tucks his tunic into his girdle and dashes toward the tomb. The boulder is already rolled away, so he enters cautiously. What he experiences takes his breath away.

Here are the empty grave clothes, but it's not the clothes that cause him to believe. It's the residue of glory that still hangs in the air. John can feel the life of God everywhere. His presence still trails behind Him. Like a sweet musky perfume, the aroma of Jesus drifts through the atmosphere of the tomb.

John returns to the upper room, puzzled but believing. The day passes quickly, the whole area of Jerusalem buzzing with news about Jesus' Resurrection.

Then, suddenly, John's heart almost stops. The whole room fills with the heavy presence of God. John looks up quickly to see what causes the stir.

Without a twist of the bolt or a turn of the knob, the Lord Himself walks through the door. "Shalom!" He says, His smile splashing glory over everyone.

John feels his knees weaken. His heart throbs hard against his chest. Tears wash his face as he sees Jesus reach out, exposing the gaping holes in His hands, His feet, His side.

The young disciple's eyes bulge as he looks into these deep, shining wounds. "Master!" breathes John, falling to his knees.

Jesus lifts His nail-scarred hands and breathes out upon them all. "Receive the Holy Spirit," He says, His eyes gleaming with love.

The young disciple closes his eyes and breathes in the life of Christ. He drinks and drinks and drinks of the sweet presence of God. His body trembles as his whole being floods with weighty glory. He knows this is the glory which Jesus died to give him. It's free to receive but it cost God everything.

Come and Drink

Wouldn't you like to draw near, like John, and drink from this overflowing fountain? Jesus drank the Father's Cup for you; now He bids you come and drink cupfuls of His resurrection glory. He invites, *"If anyone is thirsty, let him come to me and drink"* (John 7:37).

So come look back up at this *Masterpiece* and see the open wounds still carved in His flesh. Behold His love, rushing like waterfalls from His wounds. Lie down in that love. Soak yourself in it. Get on the floor, with a pillow under your head and soft worship music filling the room. Now sense the healing waters saturating your skin. Simply soak. Feel the warmth on your face. The heat in your hands.

Let the currents of His love go in deep. Reach up, as if to take the hand of God and place it over your own heart. Feel your own hand pressing down, but believe that the hand of God is pressing more. Open wide. Let His love flow in. Receive it. Drink it, for as Paul said, *"God has poured his love into our hearts by the Holy Spirit"* (Romans 5:5).[4]

Discover the wonder of soaking. Immerse your whole being in the presence of God. Now tell Him how you feel about Him. Tell Him how much you love Him. Exchange the love. He pours down on you; you pour back on Him.[5] Even as rivers always flow back to their source, let the river of love flow in and out and back up to Him.

This is the purpose for which you were created. This is why you were born. Adam lived and breathed in the glory of His presence, and you were created to do the same. You cannot exist without His presence. Life is meaningless without it. But His presence isn't just a thought; it's an experience. It's an encounter with God's *Masterpiece* of Glory.

The Victory Proclaimed

Through the years I've sometimes heard preachers say, "We need to move beyond the Cross, for it is the place of defeat; the Resurrection is the place of victory." In his book *The Cross of Christ*, John R. W. Stott corrects this misconception: "We are not to regard the cross as defeat and the resurrection as victory. Rather, the cross was the victory won, and the resurrection the victory endorsed, proclaimed and demonstrated."[6]

Do you see why I say we have forgotten the most vital part of the Easter story? We love to dress up at Easter and shout about the Resurrection, but we've forgotten what the Resurrection proclaims. The glory of the Resurrection is the glory of the Cross. That's why Paul said, *"God forbid that I should glory, save in the cross of our Lord Jesus Christ"* (Galatians 6:14).

And amazingly, once we truly allow the Cross to pierce our hearts, resurrection glory will flood us through and through. You see, the Resurrection of Jesus is the outflowing of His finished work on the Cross. When we allow the Cross to finish its work in us, we too will flow in resurrection power.

I saw this happen with our interns when they left our camp. For three months they had looked up at Jesus. Often they lay on the floor, weeping over the Lamb, sobbing over the Cup, allowing the Lord to draw His sword through their hearts.

Now they were carrying a passion for His glory that consumed them. DeHavilland, one of our staff members, called me, bubbling over with joy. "I'm completely ruined for the Lamb! Yesterday I preached on the Father's Cup in a church in New Jersey. Afterward the pastor ran up crying, 'Just last night I read the story of Jesus praying about the Cup in the garden. I asked the Lord to please give me a revelation of the Cup! Today you gave me that revelation!'"

"But, Dr. Sandy," DeHavilland continued, "the best part was what God did in the church when we prayed. Cathy, David, Brandon, and I prayed and the power of God came down! Especially on the children!" Then she said with a smile in her voice, "A precious little five-year-old girl burst out saying, 'Jesus just spoke to me and said He wants to by my Savior!'"

One of the guys said, "Dr. Sandy, it's amazing! When we preach the power of the Cross, God manifests the power of the Holy Spirit!" I kept hearing stories like this. Mandy, Lydia, and Michelle called from England, saying, "We prayed for the children in our church, and God came down on all of them!"

The same thing happened in our church here in Alabama, before the interns left.[7] When Mary and several of the interns prayed for the children, the power of God fell upon them and they were completely overcome with His presence. As they shook and laughed and wept in His glory, one little girl cried, "Toys are sometimes good, but they are the devil's tools to keep us away from God!"

You see, this is resurrection glory. It pours from the heart of the Lamb opened up on the Cross. It's not weird or flaky. It's real and it brings people into a genuine encounter with God.

Wouldn't you like to partake of this divine glory? It's not to make you rich or famous or popular. It's to make Jesus popular! It's to bring glory to the Lamb for what He suffered on the Cross! It's to reveal God's *Masterpiece!* So please pray:

Precious Jesus, there's nothing I want more than You. It's just You! I long for more of Your presence. I'm thirsty to drink of Your glory. But I don't want that glory for myself. I want it for You!

Holy Spirit, come and do Your crucifying work in my heart. Then fill me with the resurrection glory that flows from the finished work of the Cross. Let me carry Your glory to the dark places around me, displaying through my life GOD'S MASTERPIECE OF GLORY!

Endnotes

1. We don't worship the Cross, however, for it is only two stakes of wood. The Cross is symbolic of the completed work of Christ. That's why Paul wrote, *"May I never boast, except in the cross of our Lord Jesus Christ"* (Galatians 6:14). Bobby Conner in *The Cross* writes, "There is no salvation in the cross of Christ, but salvation rests in the Christ of the cross....Religion lifts up the cross, but true Christianity must lift up Christ. Let's not embrace a symbol while rejecting the Savior" (Bobby Conner, *The Cross* [Vancouver, WA: Miracle Printers, 2002], p. 14.

2. The Jewish day ends at sunset and a new day begins. Therefore Jesus was placed in the tomb before sunset on Friday—the first day. His body lay in the tomb from Friday night until Saturday night—the second day. His body is still in the tomb on the third day, which began at sunset on Saturday. It is now the early hours of the morning on the third day (Sunday), still dark outside.

3. This agreement is called by scholars The Covenant of Redemption, made between Father, Son, and Holy Spirit before creation.

4. Bob Sorge says, "Should you tap into God's divine power source, you will discover that it is a rush-flow of electric love that will drive and carry you along" (Bob Sorge, *The Fire of God's Love* [Greenwood, MI: Oasis House, 1996], p. 9).

5. Carol Arnott of Toronto says, "Soaking is positioning yourself before God to experience His love for you and to give your love to Him." Carol further says, "God wants more than a five-minute fling. It takes time and a conscious effort to prioritize what God sees as our deepest human need, the need to experience His intimate, unconditional love" (Carol Arnott, "Why I Soak," *Spread the Fire Magazine* [Toronto, ON, Canada: Toronto Airport Christian Fellowship, Issue 5, Nov. 2005], p. 4).

6. John R. W. Stott, *The Cross of Christ* (Downers Grove, IL: InterVarsity Press, 1986), p. 235.

7. The name of our church is "The Church of His Presence" in Daphne, Alabama, with Pastor John Kilpatrick.

Five

The Magnificent Masterpiece

Living for the Greatest Purpose on Earth

John's face burns with glory as he looks up at Jesus on the mount. This time, however, it's not a hill of crucifixion; it's the hill of ascension.

The Master stretches out His hands and begins to pray for His followers. John opens wide and absorbs the power flowing out from the wounds of the Lamb. Though these hands once bled from nails, now they bleed with the blessings of God.

Jesus pushes down on His feet and begins to rise. Upward He soars, still pouring out blessings as He ascends.[1] The sight before the young disciple is breathtaking. Jesus looks like a Magnificent *Masterpiece* as He mounts above the trees.

An Extravagant Expression of Love

John watches, amazed by the beauty of the Lord.

Wounds stud His flesh like medals of glory, reminding the young disciple of that day on another hill when he looked upon the Lamb.

It was the most extravagant expression of God's love ever seen in Heaven or earth. Every stroke of the Father's brush had been dipped in divine mercy, stained with His tears, and glazed with His love. For there in a little studio on a hill, God had painted His incomparable work of art. He primed it with a Roman scourge. Etched it with iron spikes. The pallet knife was a soldier's spear, and the paint was the blood of His own Son's veins.

Then the Father drenched Him with sin, blazed Him with wrath, and consumed Him in divine judgment. He buried Him in a tomb and raised Him in resurrection glory. Now He lifts Him on high to be placed in the Museum of Eternity.

If a picture speaks more than a thousand words, this portrait spoke measureless volumes. For there, captured on the canvas at Calvary, God displayed the magnitude of His love.

Words could not sufficiently express the fullness of His love, so He preached it on two pieces of wood. He dramatized it in a theater at Golgotha. He danced it on a stage at Calvary. It's like the dancer who was asked to interpret her dance. "If I could have explained it, I wouldn't have danced it," she said.

That's what God did. And though libraries are filled with books explaining the transcendent attributes of Deity, nowhere will you see God's attributes more eloquently inscribed than there on two pieces of timber.

Look closely and you'll see—compassion dripped from every tear. Mercy glowed in every blood drop. Peace and love oozed from every wound. Holiness exuded from every scar. For there, captured on the canvas at Calvary, all the attributes of God converged in one glorious blend.

All the beauties of nature could never display God's glory like His own bleeding Son. As Charles Spurgeon said, "If any creative mind desires to see the glory of God, he need not gaze upon the starry skies or soar into the heavens; he has but to bow at the foot of the cross and watch the crimson streams that gush from Immanuel's wounds."[2]

Scars Tell the Story

Yes, these wounds tell the story. They are like medallions of honor ever reminding us of the Cup Jesus drank and the victory He won. Sadly, however, many of us only see the scars and never look deeper. This leaves us with a shallow understanding of what He did. Therefore, we forget the Cross and move on to more "thrilling" subjects.

It's much like the story of Private Bill. One day Bill walked cautiously down a dirt road in Vietnam, searching for enemy soldiers who could be hiding among the civilians. As he turned a bend in the road, he saw a little hut and heard the cry of a mother. Her little girl was struggling with a Vietcong soldier. Irritated, the man reached in and pulled out a live grenade. He tossed it toward the family and ran off.

Private Bill saw the grenade, which had landed near the youngest child. Racing toward the three-year-old, he threw himself forward, pushing the child out of the way. Then he grabbed the grenade and tried to throw it, but it exploded in his hand. His arm was blown off, his right eye blinded, his right ear blown out, and half his face blown away.

That's what Jesus did for us. He threw Himself in front of God's wrath and took it on Himself. Scholars call this *propitiation*, which means, "a sacrifice that averts wrath, taking it into Himself."

You see, this is what we often miss when we only see the scars. In Heaven He still bares scars like a slain Lamb, but the scars are to point us back to His work on the Cross. The rest of Private Bill's story helps explain.

There in Vietnam medics found Bill, stopped the bleeding, and shipped him back to America for multiple surgeries. Finally he was released from the hospital with a prosthetic arm, a blind eye, and a mutilated face. And though he was honored by the Marines, the war in America was unpopular, and he was terribly dishonored by the people.

Everywhere he went, people made cruel remarks, rejecting him for participating in the war and for his hideous appearance. Often hippies pointed at him and mocked. The most painful moment was the day when a young woman on a bus spat in his face.

Depression engulfed him until he finally decided to end his own life. But before he would commit this fatal act, he would visit the land of Vietnam where, five years before, he had lost everything.

A week later he found himself wandering up a dirt path in the same little village in Vietnam. He walked along in depression, memories of the war flooding his mind. As he turned a bend in the road, he recognized the little hut where the soldier had attacked the child. As he thought of that fateful day, he sat down on a rock and buried his face in his hands.

Suddenly the cry of a teenage girl jolted him from his thoughts. He looked up to see the teenager and her brother running toward him. Behind them ran a mother and two other children. In broken English the girl asked, "S-sir, are you Private Bill?"

"Why, yes, I am. How did you know?"

"Well, sir, on the day when the grenade blew up, Americans came to carry you away. They said your name was

Private Bill and that you would live but would be very scarred." With tears sparkling in her eyes, she cried, "Sir, you're the one who saved us! For years we prayed for God to bring you back so we could thank you for the scars!"

Bill broke down weeping. In America he had only experienced rejection because of his mutilated face. Now somebody loved him for his wounds. His scars told the story of what he had done for them.

That's just like Jesus. His scars tell the story of what He did for us. Even as Private Bill took the full impact of the grenade on himself, Jesus took the full exploding impact of God's judgment on Himself. Now He still bears scars to remind us of His sacrifice. His wounds reveal to us God's *Masterpiece.*

The Mark of the Cross

An ancient legend calls every person to make the mark of the Cross somewhere on the earth before he or she dies. Won't you let God use you to make this mark of the Cross somewhere in your world?

When Ryan left our camp several years ago, he carried the mark of the Cross in his heart. He radiated so much passion for Jesus that just meeting him made Brandon desperately hungry. Because he wanted what he saw in Ryan, he came out to our internship in Alabama.

One day in our "Glory of the Lamb" class, Brandon said,

"I saw a picture of myself burning in hell. I was wailing on the floor, and calling out to the Lamb. I cried out with all my heart, 'Pierce me, Lord!'" It's what happened next that changed him forever. "Then I felt His sword go through me. Like Isaiah, I was so undone. I was bleeding but I also had joy because I knew what God was doing. I said, 'God, if I don't preach the Cross, take me home.'"…

I want to make it to the end, preaching and giving glory to the Lamb for His reward!"

Another student, Aisha, came to me on the last day before she went back to England. When she first came here, she was so shy and hurt inside that she refused to eat. But Jesus healed her at the Cross and even made a preacher out of her.[3] With sincerity shining in her eyes, she said, "Dr. Sandy, the Lord told me to tell you—I have promised God that for the rest of my life I will preach only Jesus Christ and Him crucified!"

What about you? Will you let God use you to make the mark of the Cross in the world? Will you tell about God's *Masterpiece* and bring Jesus His reward? This is the greatest purpose on earth.

But you say, "I can't speak." Then say it without words. Paint it on a canvas. Write it in a book. Portray it in a drama, a song, a movie, a dance. Express it by giving cups of living water to the poor and the broken. That's what God did, and He asks you to do the same.

One Final Glimpse

A sense of awe and reverence sweeps over the young disciple. Like Moses long ago, he feels he should remove the shoes from his feet. God's presence is everywhere.

John squints his eyes to see the Lord as He rises higher and higher. Then a cloud comes and blocks his view. The disciple turns to leave, but he feels too weak to walk. His heart is too full to speak. He simply drops to his knees, closes his eyes, and worships. As he lifts his praise to Jesus, he can almost see Him as *"a Lamb, looking as if it had been slain"* (Revelation 5:6).

We leave John now, but you can read the rest of the story in my book *The Glory of the Lamb*.[4] Here the old apostle, now in chains on the Island of Patmos, looks into Heaven and beholds the Lamb of God. From the high hill of his old age, he unfolds *The Glory of the Lamb* from Eternity past to Eternity future.

Now as the young John kneels and worships, he bows his head and whispers the only words that can describe what he has seen. With the seraphim around the throne, he simply whispers, "Holy, holy, holy…."

For this is God's Magnificent *Masterpiece*. This is indeed the axis on which both time and eternity revolve. It is the nucleus of the Christian faith, the pith and marrow of the Gospel. It is the focus of angels, the central attraction of the seraphim, the fountainhead of glory, the lamp of all Heaven.

All the past flows into this glorious work of art. All the future pours out from it. The Resurrection proclaims it. The Ascension displays it. The Bible chronicles it. All revival flows from it.[5] This is God's finest work. This is His Magnum Opus, His Magnificent *Masterpiece*.

He Will Be Unveiled

One night, Mary, head of our internship, cried out with heart-shaking passion. "Often I've found myself on the floor weeping in a church after I've listened to a sermon. I'm not thinking I could do better; I'm weeping for the Lamb to receive glory!" Then her voice rose as she cried, "The Father is determined for His Son to be lifted up, and He will not end this age until the Lamb is glorified on this earth!"

Mary is right, for the Father aches to see His Beloved Son receive the honor and glory He deserves. All Heaven gives Him that glory, as they cry *"Worthy is the Lamb,"* but what about us on earth?

And though the world may shake with impending disasters, it is only to bring about God's purposes on this globe. God's Son will be revealed again as the Lamb. He will become the central focus of His church on earth even as He is in Heaven. And He will receive the full reward of

His suffering. Easter's forgotten glory will be revealed. God's Magnificent *Masterpiece* will at last be unveiled!

So, as you lay this book aside, won't you drop to your knees, look back up to the Lamb, and pray:

O God, please use me to tell them! In the schools, in the streets, in the church, in my family – let me tell them what Your Son did. I will tell them about the Cup of wrath He drank on the Cross. I will tell them about the fires of hell He endured. I will tell them about His triumphant victory at Calvary, and I will walk in the authority He died to give me.

Father, for the rest of my life I resolve to bring Your Son the reward of His suffering. I promise I will tell others about this neglected truth in the Gospel. I have found the greatest purpose on earth and I will live my whole life to reveal THE MASTERPIECE OF GOD!

Endnotes

1. Still pouring blessings, Luke 24:51 says, *"While he was blessing them, he left them and was taken up into heaven."*

2. Charles Spurgeon, "Mourning at the Sight of the Crucified," *The Power of the Cross of Christ*, Lance Wubbels, comp. (Lynnwood, WA: Emerald Books, 1995), p. 192.

3. In our preaching class, young adults and teenagers, many of whom had never preached, learned how to find their "preaching voice." We saw students become amazing preachers in just three months.

4. In the *Glory of the Lamb* (McDougal Publishing, 2002), John the Apostle, while gazing on Christ's glory in Heaven, reflects back on the glory before creation, creation's glory, the glory through the Old Testament, the glory of Christ's life, the glory of Gethesemane and the Cross, the resurrection and ascension glory, and Christ's glorification in Heaven. You can order this book from any Christian or secular bookstore or on the Internet.

   Also be watching next Christmas for my new book, *The Highest Glory of Christmas,* as Mary, the mother of Jesus, tells her story of Jesus and the Cross.

5. My next book is entitled *The Unquenchable Flame* with the subtitle, *How to Keep the Fires of Revival Burning Continually*. It reveals why revivals burn out if the Cross is no longer preached. Even as God told Moses to never let the fires go out on the altar of burnt offering (Leviticus 6:9-13), God tells us never let the fires of revival burn out. The only way to keep the fire of revival burning continually is to keep the Burnt Offering Himself — the Lamb of God — in the center of revival.

Other Books by Sandy Kirk

The Glory of the Lamb
1-158158-074-6

A Revelation of the Lamb
1-158158-063-0

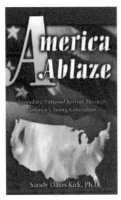

America Ablaze
1-158158-053-3

Rivers of Glory
1-158158-053-3

You may order these books by going to
www.mcdougalpublishing.com or calling 301.797.6637.

GLORY CAMPS FOR YOUTH

Camp America Ablaze — Outside Pensacola, FL

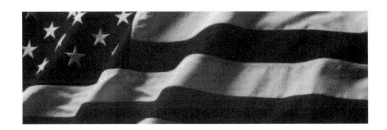

Youth Pastors, bring your young adults, teens, or children to Camp America Ablaze to receive impartations of Revival Fire and the Glory of the Cross!

We will schedule a camp to meet your plans. Enjoy the beautiful beaches of the Gulf Coast as well as our facility with lighted basketball and tennis court, football/soccer field, baseball field, swimming pool, prayer garden, horse-shoes, and sand volleyball court.

E-mail Dr. Sandy (campablaze@juno.com)
or call (251-962-7172)
See the website for more info:
www.campamericaablaze.com